ARTIFICIAL INTELLIGENCE, A WAY FORWARD FOR THE LEGAL PROFESSION?

WALIAT JIMOH

ISBN: 9798351293493

DEDICATION

This Research is dedicated to my Family for their consistent support and uneding sacrifices

CONTENTS

1. TITLE PAGE
2. COPYRIGHT
3. DEDICATION
4. ABSTRACT
5. INTRODUCTION
6. BENEFITS OF ARTIFICIAL INTELLIGENCE TO LEGAL PROFESSION
7. SCOPE

4

ABSTRACT

Technology is fast emerging in the Fourth Industrial Revolution world and becoming one of the major requirements to advance professions in their various fields. Artificial Intelligence has enormous advantages than it is perceived to be and a much greater opportunity to offer to the legal profession if it is leveraged. This write-up seeks to evaluate the importance of Artificial intelligence to the legal profession and how it can be leveraged to enable a significant breakthrough in legal practice. It also seeks to outline the various forms of artificial intelligence, as well as the various challenges posed to the legal profession, should artificial intelligence not be leveraged. This paper also seeks to accentuate the inevitability of technology glaring right at not just the corporate sector but also at individuals. Artificial Intelligence cannot overtake the position of a lawyer because it is merely a tool designed to make tasks easier and faster, it also needs human intervention and supervision to function. In recent times, the use of Artificial Intelligence has enabled lawyers to develop the requisite skills to perform efficiently in the emerging technological world. Hence, only innovative law firms can keep up with the new form of legal practice.

5
INTRODUCTION

The term 'Artificial Intelligence' can be applied to computer systems that are intended to replicate human cognitive functions. In particular, Artificial Intelligence can also be referred to as Machine learning or cognitive computing. 'Machine Learning, where algorithms detect patterns in data, and apply these new patterns to automate certain tasks.[1] Artificial intelligence mimics certain operations of the human mind and is the term used when machines are able to complete tasks that typically require human intelligence. The term machine learning is when computers use rules (algorithms) to analyze data and learn patterns and glean insights from the data. Artificial intelligence is a large factor in shifting the way legal work is done.[2] Artificial Intelligence can be referred to as the duplication of human intelligence into a machine in a way that programs the machine able to think and perform like humans to an extent. According to the Oxford Dictionary, Artificial Intelligence is a wide-ranging branch of computers concerned with building smart machines capable of performing tasks that typically require human intelligence such as visual perception, speech recognition, decision making, and translation between languages. According to

Deloitte, 100,000 legal roles will be automated by 2036. They report that by 2020 law firms will be faced with a "tipping point" for a new talent strategy. AI-powered software improves the efficiency of document analysis for legal use and machines can review documents and flag them as relevant to a particular case. Once a certain type of document is denoted as relevant, machine learning algorithms can get to work to find other documents that are similarly relevant. Machines are much faster at sorting through documents than humans and can produce output and results that can be statistically validated. They can help reduce the load on the human workforce by forwarding only documents that are questionable rather than requiring humans to review all documents. It's important that legal research is done in a timely and comprehensive manner, even though it's monotonous. AI systems such as the one offered by ROSS Intelligence leverage natural language processing to help analyze documents.[3] There are many types of artificial intelligence including machine learning, where instead of being programmed with what to think, machines can observe, analyze and learn from data and mistakes just like our human brains can. This technology is influencing consumer products and has led to significant breakthroughs in healthcare and physics as well as altered industries as diverse as manufacturing, finance, and retail. In part due to the tremendous amount of data we generate every day and the computing power available, artificial intelligence has exploded in recent years. We might still be years away from generalized AI when a machine can do anything a human brain can do, but AI in its current form is still an essential part of our world.[4] It is noteworthy that artificial intelligence is not programmed to replace humans as it cannot entirely function without human intervention. Burnett (2016) also argues that the introduction of Artificial intelligence means that fewer people will be required to do lower-skilled, transactional work leading to a smaller base at the bottom. Solicitors will no longer be gaining skills and judgment by working their way up through the ranks. How will they gain these skills? How will leaders of the future be developed? How can the experience and judgment of senior people (which is needed to train

AI systems) be captured before they retire?[5] AI has a cogent role in upgrading the legal sector. it will become a vital tool for Lawyers to become relevant and more competitive than usual. The use of Artificial Intelligence will enable a lawyer to develop the requisite skills to perform efficiently in the emerging technological world. Firms that fail to take advantage of AI-powered efficiencies may lag in competing with those who do at least to the extent clients insist on fixed-rate billing. Thus, lawyers who understand technology, and educate themselves about the latest legal tech developments. may be of increasing value to their firms.[6]

EXAMPLES OF ARTIFICIAL INTELLIGENCE

1. Google Map
2. Siri
3. Digital Assistant
4. Ride-sharing Apps such as Uber, Lyft, Taxify, and so on
5. Face detection and recognition
6. Autocorrect and spell checkers
7. Social Media Monitoring
8. Chatbots

6

ADVANTAGES OF ARTIFICIAL INTELLIGENCE

Artificial Intelligence has been programmed to with numerous potentials to serve humans in their various fields, some of these advantages include; productivity. It saves time. It improves accuracy and speed and Encourages proficiency

BENEFITS OF ARTIFICIAL INTELLIGENCE TO THE LEGAL PROFESSION.

Artificial Intelligence is not doomsday for the legal profession. Instead, AI has a cogent role in upgrading the legal sector. it will become a vital tool for Lawyers to become relevant and more competitive than usual. The use of Artificial Intelligence will enable lawyers to develop requisite skills to perform efficiently in the emerging technological world, some of the benefits that can be derived from leveraging on A.I includes:

1. Organizational structure reform
2. Due diligence review
3. Risk assessment
4. Document analysis
5. Reduction of ambiguity and complexity

1. ORGANIZATIONAL STRUCTURE REFORM

Law firms that leverage on the use of artificial intelligence will have an advanced organizational structure that will enhance efficiency. This new technology will help to provide better services and be highly skilled for client management. The use of technology in daily proceedings will enable easier and faster administration which will help solve the challenges of slow proceedings and as a result create rooms to accelerate productivity.

2. DUE DILIGENCE REVIEW

Lawyers are tasked to exercise due diligence in their daily proceedings such as adequate preparation of document data by analyzing the documents and ensuring that the required documents are made available when needed. However, the use of Artificial Intelligence to achieve due diligence will enable Lawyers to mitigate the stress by automating the search of required documents. Artificial intelligence will also enable the easier and faster by analyzing data and converting it to a preferred format. Artificial intelligence can also help to sort document data either by name or by date of entry thereby making due diligence less cumbersome.

3. RISK ASSESSMENT

A deficiency in risk assessment could result in expensive lawsuits to the detriment of both the lawyer and the client, Artificial intelligence is capable of helping Lawyers to review assessments as well as identify risks that are likely to pose threats to the smooth running of their proceedings. In the instance of lawsuits, the availability of AI-driven applications will help law firms and lawyers discover information and data that need optimal protection quickly. The progress of competent risk assessment will enable law firms and lawyers to correctly assess risk outcomes while minimizing costs and protecting their reputations and clients.

4. DOCUMENT ANALYSIS

Another duty of a lawyer is to make research on their cases in order to Artificial intelligence will enable lawyer to research qualitatively in the most sophisticated way. The use of artificial intelligence will enable automated document review by simply searching for the documents rather than going through a mountain of files that makes the job tiresome.

5. REDUCTION OF AMBIGUITY AND COMPLEXITY

Artificial Intelligence such as spell checker and autocorrect is capable of helping lawyers to avoid ambiguity and also review and eliminate errors contained in a document.

LIMITATIONS OF ARTIFICIAL INTELLIGENCE

Despite the numerous advantages that can be derived from the use of Arizona intelligence there are limits to what AI can do. According to Yuen Thio, AI can't yet replicate advocacy, negotiation, or structuring of complex deals. The New York Times suggested that tasks like advising clients, writing briefs, negotiating deals, and appearing in court were beyond the reach of computerization, at least for a while. AI also isn't yet very good at the type of creative writing in a Supreme Court brief or a movie script. The work of lawyers, especially junior associates, will involve identifying and understanding data ready for processing, review the results, and make necessary changes. As a result, there will be a higher premium on understanding clients' intention and framework than the current emphasis on drafting technique. Furthermore, artificial Intelligence can not overtake the position of a lawyer because it is merely a tool designed to make tasks easier and faster, it also needs human intervention and supervision to function. In conclusion, Artificial Intelligence has enormous advantages than it is perceived to be and a much greater opportunity to offer to the legal profession if it is leveraged. It should be seen as more of an innovation than a threat or a problem. It is here to not only stay but also make legal practice more prestigious than it is, improve the values of lawyers, and make them more competitive. It is safe to say that Law firms that do not adopt the use of artificial intelligence in this 21st century will become obsolete, irrelevant and unproductive to legal service.

RESEARCH QUESTION

The Research seeks to answer the following questions: Would Artificial Intelligence have an impact on the Legal Profession?

Does the Legal Profession need to leverage Artificial Intelligence?

Can the Legal Profession make use of Artificial Intelligence in judicial processes?

HYPOTHESIS

The following are the hypothesis to be derived from the research: Artificial Intelligence would have a great impact on the Legal Profession.

The Legal Profession needs to leverage Artificial Intelligence.

The Legal Profession can make use of Artificial Inspiration in judicial processes

OBJECTIVE OF THE STUDY

The main aim of the research is to examine the effect of Artificial Intelligence on the legal field, it seeks to establish the facts that the use of Artificial Intelligence will achieve due diligence as it enables Lawyers to mitigate stress by automating the search of required documents. The research also seeks to establish the fact that Law firms that leverage the use of artificial intelligence will have an advanced organizational structure that will enhance efficiency. This new technology will help to provide better services and be highly skilled in client management. The use of technology in daily proceedings will enable easier and faster administration which will help solve the challenges of slow proceedings and as a result create rooms to accelerate productivity. Artificial intelligence is capable of helping Lawyers to review assessments as well as identify risks that are likely to pose threats to the smooth running of their proceedings. In the instance of lawsuits, the availability of AI-driven applications will help law firms and lawyers discover information and data that need optimal protection quickly. The progress of competent risk assessment will enable law firms and lawyers to correctly assess risk outcomes while minimizing costs and protecting their reputations and clients.[7]

ARTIFICIAL INTELLIGENCE, A WAY FORWARD FOR THE LEGAL PROFESSION?

CONTRIBUTION TO KNOWLEDGE

Artificial Intelligence has enormous advantages than it is perceived to be and a much greater opportunity to offer to the legal profession if it is leveraged. It should be seen as more of an innovation than a threat or a problem. It is here to not only stay but also make legal practice more prestigious than it is, improve the values of lawyers, and make them more competitive. It is safe to say that Law firms that do not adopt the use of artificial intelligence in this 21st century will become obsolete, irrelevant, and unproductive to legal services it can be stated that adoption of Artificial Intelligence will lead to a reduction of ambiguity and complexity that is various forms of artificial intelligence such as spell checker and autocorrect are capable of helping lawyers to avoid ambiguity and also review and eliminate errors contained in a document.

ARTIFICIAL INTELLIGENCE, A WAY FORWARD FOR THE LEGAL PROFESSION?

RESEARCH METHODOLOGY

The methodology consists of the procedure and instruments that were used to collect data for this study. It explains the research instruments and methods that were used in implementing the aforementioned objectives in the study to be adopted on this research. The research methodology to be adopted will be carried out through the use of secondary sources such as study materials and quantitative research. Furthermore, the data collection will be carried out through documents and records, case studies, interviews, questionnaires, and observation. The tools of analysis will be carried out through a doctrinal approach that is, textual analysis.

7

SCOPE

This research focuses specifically on Artificial Intelligence, its forms, and its benefits such as time-saving, enabling proficiency, speed, and accuracy. It also seeks to establish how it can improve and enhance the legal profession in areas of Risk assessments, due diligence review, data analysis, and organizational structure reform. Furthermore, it's stated the limitations of Artificial Intelligence that is, despite the numerous advantages that can be derived from the use of Arizona intelligence there are limits to what AI can do. According to Yuen Thio, AI can't yet replicate advocacy, negotiation, or structuring of complex deals. The New York Times suggested that tasks like advising clients, writing briefs, negotiating deals, and appearing in court were beyond the reach of computerization, at least for a while. AI also isn't yet very good at the type of creative writing in a Supreme Court brief. Or a movie script.[8] The work of lawyers, especially junior associates, will involve identifying and understanding data ready for processing, reviewing the results, and making necessary changes. As a result, there will be a higher premium on understanding clients' intentions and frameworks than the current emphasis on drafting techniques. Furthermore, artificial Intelligence can not overtake the position of a lawyer because it is merely a tool designed to make tasks easier and faster, it also needs human intervention and supervision to function.

ARTIFICIAL INTELLIGENCE, A WAY FORWARD FOR THE LEGAL PROFESSION?

REFERENCES

[1] https://www.academia.edu/36920594/Artificial_Intelligence_and_the_Legal_Profession <accessed on 12th May 2021>

[2] Available at https://bernardmarr.com/default.asp?contentID=1464

[3] Available at https://bernardmarr.com/default.asp?contentID=1464

[4] Bernard Marr 'What is the importance of Artificial Intelligence ' Retrieved from: https://bernardmarr.com/default.asp?contentID=1829

[5] Burnett, Sarah(2016), 'Legally AI – Disruption in legal services and beyond'. Retrieved from:

https://www.professionaloutsourcingmagazine.net/insight/legally-ai-disruption-in-legal-services-and-beyond

[6] https://jolt.law.harvard.edu/digest/a-primer-on-using-artificial-intelligence-in-the-legal-profession

<accessed on 16th May 2021>

[7] Avaneesh Marwaha, Seven Benefits of Artificial Intelligence For Law Firms, Law Technology Today, July 2017, https://www.lawtechnologytoday.org/2017/07/seven-benefits-artificial-intelligence-law-firms/

[8] https://jolt.law.harvard.edu/digest/a-primer-on-using-artificial-intelligence-in-the-legal-profession <accessed on 13th May 2021

www.ingramcontent.com/pod-product-compliance
Lightning Source LLC
LaVergne TN
LVHW052116160826
845678LV00015B/3588

* 9 7 9 8 3 5 1 2 9 3 4 9 3 *